Best Easy Day Hikes Series

Best Easy Day Hikes
Albuquerque

Bruce Grubbs

FALCON GUIDES

GUILFORD, CONNECTICUT
HELENA, MONTANA
AN IMPRINT OF GLOBE PEQUOT PRESS

FALCONGUIDES®

TOPO! Explorer software and SuperQuad source maps courtesy of
National Geographic Maps. For information about TOPO! Explorer,
TOPO!, and Nat Geo Maps products, go to www.topo.com or www
.natgeomaps.com.

Maps by Bruce Grubbs © Morris Book Publishing, LLC

Library of Congress Cataloging-in-Publication Data
Grubbs, Bruce (Bruce O.)
  Best easy day hikes, Albuquerque / Bruce Grubbs.
    p. cm. – (FalconGuides)
  ISBN 978-0-7627-5149-5
  1. Hiking–New Mexico–Albuquerque Region–Guidebooks. 2. Albu-
querque Region (N.M.)–Guidebooks. I. Title.
  GV199.42.N62A438 2009
  917.89'61–dc22

                                                        2009029484

Printed in the United States of America
10 9 8 7 6 5 4 3 2 1

Contents

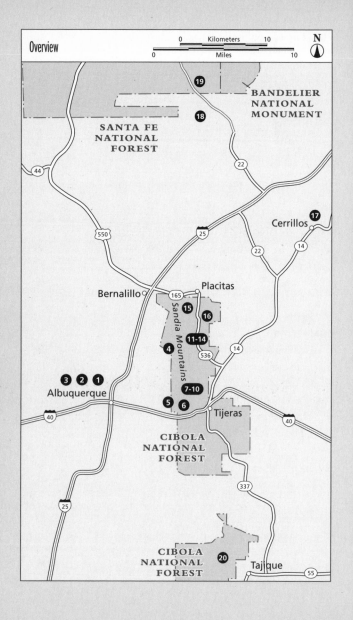

Overview

Kilometers
0   10
Miles
0   10

N

BANDELIER
NATIONAL
MONUMENT

SANTA FE
NATIONAL
FOREST

44

550

25

22

22

14

Cerrillos

17

19

18

Bernalillo

Placitas

165

15

16

11-14

4

536

14

3 2 1

Albuquerque

7-10

40

5 6

Tijeras

40

Sandia Mountains

CIBOLA
NATIONAL
FOREST

337

25

CIBOLA
NATIONAL
FOREST

20

Tajique

55

Acknowledgments

Special thanks to Diane Souder, Petroglyphs National Monument, for reviewing the manuscript. I would like to thank my many hiking companions down the years who've put up with my incessant trail mapping and photography. Thanks to Duart Martin for her support and encouragement. And finally, thanks to my editors at Globe Pequot Press, Scott Adams and John Burbidge, for making a book out of my rough manuscript.

Introduction

New Mexico, the Land of Enchantment, is certainly
enchanted for hikers. The mountains, mesas, and canyons
of this rugged state offer a great variety of hikes. Sometimes,
though, you don't want to drive long distances to enjoy a
hike. Luckily for residents and visitors in the state's largest
metropolitan area, Albuquerque, there is plenty of hiking
near the city.

This guide lists easy to moderate hikes within 90 miles
of Albuquerque. Some of the hikes lie within the city itself,
while many are in the Sandia Mountains. Other hikes are
in the nearby Manzano Mountains and the hills and mesas
north of the city.

The premier Albuquerque hiking destination, the Sandia
Mountains, dominates the eastern skyline and rises more
than 5,000 feet in a series of steep slopes and rock buttresses
to the 10,000-foot Sandia Crest. Belying the rugged appear-
ance of the western escarpment of the Sandias, the crest and
eastern slopes are gentle, forested slopes. Dozens of trails
climb or contour along the slopes, and the Crest Trail runs
the length of the range from south to north.

The mountains around Albuquerque are part of the
northern Mexican Highlands and were created by the
gigantic mountain-building forces unleashed during the
formation of the North American continent. Numerous
north-tending fractures, or faults, formed as the rocks broke
under the strain. Some of the resulting blocks sank to form
the valleys, while others rose to form the mountains. As the
faulting continues to lower the basins and raise the mountains, erosion from water flowing downhill tends to wear

1

down the mountains and fill the valleys. The topography we see today reflects the fact that the faulting is still active enough to keep the mountains from being worn down to a flat plain.

Hazards

Dehydration
Even in the mountains, where the summer air is cool, dehydration is a serious concern. Because the humidity is usually very low, your body loses moisture insensibly. Carry and drink plenty of water, and eat high-energy snacks for fuel and to help keep your electrolytes in balance. Both these measures are necessary to prevent heat exhaustion, which can develop into life-threatening sunstroke.

Plants and Animals
Various plants and animals can pose hazards to hikers in the New Mexico desert and mountains. Plants that are hazardous to the touch include poison ivy and stinging nettle. Spiny plants like cactus are easy to avoid. Never eat any plant unless you know what you are doing. Many common plants, especially mushrooms, are deadly.

Animals will normally leave you alone unless molested or provoked. Never feed wild animals, as they rapidly get used to the handouts and then will vigorously defend their new food source.

Rattlesnakes cause concern but can easily be avoided. They usually warn off intruders by rattling well before you reach striking range. Since rattlesnakes can strike no farther than half their body length, avoid placing your hands and feet in areas you cannot see, and walk several feet away from rock overhangs and shady ledges. Snakes prefer surfaces at about 80°F, so during hot weather they prefer the shade of bushes or rock overhangs, and in cool weather will be found sunning themselves on open ground.

Mosquitoes are occasionally around in small numbers after snowmelt at the higher elevations. Spring rains can sometimes bring out a few mosquitoes in the desert. Because mosquitoes can transmit West Nile virus, use repellent and sleep in a tent when they are present. DEET in various concentrations seems to be the most effective repellent.

Africanized bees, originally released in South America, have spread north and are now well established in the New Mexico deserts. Avoid all concentrations of bees, especially hives and swarms. If attacked, drop your pack and run. Protect your eyes and don't swat at the bees. Try to get into brush or dense foliage, which confuses the bees.

Old mines and prospects are common in these mountains. While hazardous areas are supposed to be signed and fenced, in practice this doesn't always happen, and some people ignore the warnings and get hurt or killed every year. Vertical shafts are a serious hazard, especially in brushy areas. Use a flashlight when walking through brushy areas at night off trail, even around camp. Never approach the edge of a pit or shaft; the edges are often unstable or undercut, and there's no way to tell how deep they are. Stay out of horizontal shafts and mines in general. They are often unstable, there can be partially covered or hidden vertical shafts, and poisonous or radioactive gasses may be present.

Weather

As a desert region, New Mexico's weather is stable for long periods. Even during the winter, when storms drop snow on the high peaks and rain on the desert floor, long periods of clear weather are the rule rather than the exception. Desert hiking is especially fine during the winter, when the mountaintops are buried in snow. Spring and fall are normally dry and offer the best weather for hiking at all elevations. After wet winters, spring often brings fantastic displays of wildflowers to the desert. When the heat of summer blasts the desert, it is best to either hike early in the morning or retreat to the alpine trails of the Spring Mountains. Late summer brings a second wet period, the North American Monsoon, an influx of seasonal moisture from the Gulf of Mexico. Later summer mornings usually dawn clear, but by noon towering cumulus clouds usually form over the mountains and develop into massive thunderstorms. Plan summer hikes to be off exposed ridges and summits by noon to avoid the thunderstorm hazards of lightning, high wind, and hail.

The best source for up-to-date weather information is the National Weather Service in Albuquerque; their Web site is www.srh.noaa.gov/abq. Commercial weather sources concentrate on urban areas and highway corridors, but by using the National Weather Service Web site, you can click on a map and get a specific point forecast for the trail you plan to hike. This is important because the weather in the mountains is usually much different than the weather in the city.

Gear Every Hiker Should Carry

- Water
- Food
- Sun hat
- Sunscreen
- Sunglasses

- Durable hiking shoes or boots
- Synthetic fleece jacket or pullover
- Rain gear
- Map
- Compass
- First-aid kit
- Signal mirror
- Toilet paper and zippered plastic bag

Environmental Considerations

The desert is a fragile environment that deserves our utmost care and respect. Please adhere to some simple practices when hiking and camping in the desert.

Stay on the trail. Don't cut switchbacks. It takes more effort and increases erosion. You will encounter mountain bikers outside designated wilderness areas. Since they're less maneuverable than you, it's polite to step aside so the riders can pass without having to veer off the trail.

Be careful with fires. Smokers should stop at a bare spot or rock ledge, then make certain that all smoking materials are out before continuing. Due to fire hazard, it may be illegal to smoke while traveling. Never smoke or light any kind of fire on windy days or when the fire danger is high, because wildfires can start easily and spread explosively.

Control your pet. Although dogs are allowed in most of the areas covered by this book, it is your responsibility to keep them from barking and bothering wildlife or other hikers. In national forests, dogs must be kept under control and on a leash when required.

Respect the environment. Don't cut live trees or plants of any kind, carve on trees or rocks, pick wildflowers, or build structures such as rock campfire rings.

Share the trail. Many of the trails in this book are open to horseback riders as well as hikers, and some are open to mountain bikers as well. Horses always have the right-of-way over hikers and cyclists, both of which should move off the trail downhill and remain still until the horses have passed. Talking quietly to the riders helps convince the horses that you are a person and not some weird monster with a hump on its back. Don't make sudden movements or noises.

Technically, hikers have the right-of-way over cyclists, but in practice it's more reasonable for hikers to step off the trail so as to avoid forcing the riders off trail. On their part, cyclists should be courteous, always ride under control, and warn hikers of their approach.

Remember that motorized vehicles and bicycles, including mountain bikes, are prohibited on trails in wilderness areas and national monuments.

Sanitation

A short walk in any popular recreation area will show you that few people seem to know how to answer the call of nature away from facilities. Diseases such as Giardiasis are spread by poor human sanitation. If facilities are available, use them. In the backcountry, select a site at least 100 yards from streams, lakes, springs, and dry washes. Avoid barren, sandy soil, if possible. Next, dig a small "cat-hole" about 6 inches down into the organic layer of the soil. (Some people carry a small plastic trowel for this purpose.) When finished, refill the hole, covering any toilet paper.

As far as trash goes, if you carried it in, you can also carry it out. Do not bury food or trash. Animals will dig it up. Never feed wild creatures. They become dependent on human food, which can lead to unpleasant encounters and cause the animal to starve during the off-season.

Three Falcon Zero-Impact Principles

- Leave with everything you brought.
- Leave no sign of your visit.
- Leave the landscape as you found it.

How to Use This Book

This book is broken into several sections, covering hikes in the city and the western foothills of the Sandia Mountains, the west slopes and the crest of the Sandia Mountains, and several other areas north and south of the city.

Using the Trail Descriptions

Each hike in the book has a number and name. Some trails have more than one common name, and other hikes use more than one trail to complete a loop or otherwise create a more interesting route. In each case, I've attempted to name the hike for the best-known trail or feature. Each hike starts with a general description of the highlights and attractions. A summary of the hike follows, with at-a-glance information.

Distance: This is the total mileage of the hike. For out-and-back hikes, it includes the return mileage. Loop hikes include the total distance around the loop. Some loops may have an out-and-back section, or cherry stem. I've selected hikes that do not require a car shuttle, for simplicity and so that you can spend more of your hiking time on the trail instead of in a car. Distances were measured on digital topographic maps and may vary slightly from official mileages but are consistent through the book.

Approximate hiking time: This is based on an average hiker who is reasonably fit. More casual hikers should allow more time. The hiking time does not include time for lunch stops, wildlife view stops, photography, or other distractions. Plan on more time for such activities. Groups should remember that the party travels at the speed of the slowest member.

Difficulty: All hikes in this book are rated easy or moderate. There are no strenuous or difficult hikes in the book, but sections of trails may be steep, rough, or otherwise more strenuous than the overall rating would indicate. Just about anyone should be able to do an easy hike. Moderate hikes require a bit of fitness, and beginners should allow extra time.

Trail surface: The type of tread you'll be walking on.

Best season: Although most hikes can be done any time of the year, this section lists the best season when temperatures and weather are at their most enjoyable. Low elevation hikes in the Albuquerque area and the foothills of the Sandia Mountains are generally best hiked from fall through spring because of the extremely hot desert summers. During the summer, higher elevation hikes in the Sandias are preferable. If you hike at low elevation during the summer, get an early start and take plenty of water.

Water availability: Although day hikers should carry all the water they need, this section lists known water sources for emergency use. All water should be purified before use.

Other trail users: These may include equestrians and mountain bikers.

Canine compatibility: Dogs are generally allowed in the state parks and national forests but must be under voice control or on a leash. This is just common courtesy to other hikers, some of whom may have had bad experiences with dogs. If your dog barks or runs up to other hikers, even in a friendly way, your dog is not under control and you are giving dog owners a bad name. Also, clean up after your dog.

Fees and permits: Entrance fees and permits required, if any, are listed here.

Maps: Each hike has a map showing the trail and any pertinent landmarks. Hikers wishing to explore further, or off trail, should carry the US Geological Survey topographic maps as listed here. These are the most detailed maps for terrain and natural features but do not show all trails.

Trail contacts: This section lists the name, address, phone number, and Web site of the managing agency. It's a good idea to contact the agency for up-to-date trail information before your hike.

Finding the trailhead: GPS coordinates in UTM are given for all trailheads. Make sure your GPS is set to the WGS84 datum. Trailhead directions are from the junction of I-40 and I-25 in Albuquerque.

The hike: This is a narrative description of the hike route and attractions you'll find along the way. There are also descriptions of relevant natural or human history.

Miles and directions: This table lists the key points, such as trail intersections or turning points on a cross-country hike, by miles and tenths. You should be able to find the route with this table alone. The mileages in this book do not necessarily agree with distances found on trails signs, agency mileages, and other descriptions because trail miles are measured by a variety of methods and personnel. All mileages in this book were carefully measured using digital topographic mapping software for accuracy and consistency.

Trail Finder

Best Hikes for Geology Lovers

Best Hikes for Children

Best Hikes for Dogs

Best Hikes for Great Views

Best Hikes for Photographers

Best Hikes for Canyons

Best Hikes for Nature Lovers

Map Legend

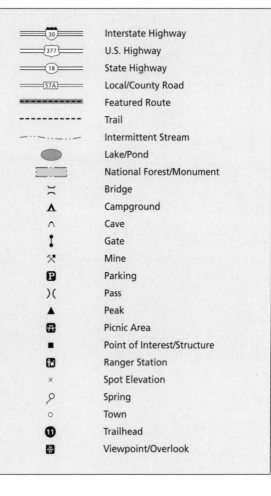

══ 30 ══	Interstate Highway
══ 377 ══	U.S. Highway
══ 18 ══	State Highway
══ 57A ══	Local/County Road
▬▬▬▬▬	Featured Route
- - - - -	Trail
⌐⌐⌐⌐	Intermittent Stream
⬭	Lake/Pond
▭	National Forest/Monument
⌣	Bridge
▲	Campground
∧	Cave
!	Gate
⚒	Mine
P	Parking
)(	Pass
▲	Peak
⛱	Picnic Area
■	Point of Interest/Structure
🏠	Ranger Station
×	Spot Elevation
ρ	Spring
○	Town
⓫	Trailhead
▣	Viewpoint/Overlook

Urban Hikes

There are many hiking opportunities in or next to the city of Albuquerque. The primary destination is Petroglyph National Monument, which sprawls over the mesa lands on the west side of the city. The national monument protects thousands of petroglyphs that are found along the mesa's eastern rim. It also encompasses an area of volcanoes west of the city. This section also includes hikes on the west side of the Sandia Mountains that are accessed from the city.

1 Rio Grande Nature Center

This loop hike takes you through part of the Rio Grande bosque, the riverside riparian zone that contains a wide variety of water-loving plant and animal life.

Distance: 2.0-mile lollipop
Approximate hiking time: 1 hour
Difficulty: Easy
Trail surface: Dirt and rocks
Best season: Fall through spring
Water availability: None
Other trail users: Mountain bikers on the access trail
Canine compatibility: Dogs on leashes allowed

Fees and permits: Entrance fee
Maps: USGS: Los Griegos
Trail contacts: Rio Grande Nature Center State Park, 2901 Candelaria Rd., Albuquerque 87107; (505) 344-7240; www.emnrd .state.nm.us/PRD/RGNC.htm
Special considerations: During the summer, hike early in the day and carry plenty of water.

Finding the trailhead: From the junction of I-40 and I-25, drive 2.1 miles west on I-40, then exit at Rio Grande Boulevard NW. Drive 1.6 miles, and then turn left onto Candelaria Road NW and drive 0.5 mile west to the park. GPS: UTM 13S 346640E 3888699N

The Hike

From the parking area, take the access trail directly west across the bridge over the riverside drain. The riverside trail starts here as a loop that can be walked either direction. Several short spurs lead to the river. After walking the loop, return to the parking area via the access trail.

The bosque, partly wooded with cottonwood trees and partly open sand flats, is a fall and winter stop for migrating waterfowl, including sandhill cranes, Canada geese, and

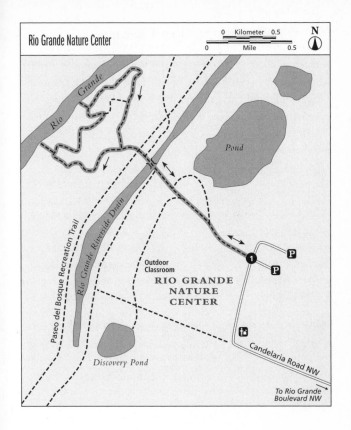

several types of ducks. Year-round residents include beaver, coyotes, and raccoons. The Rio Grande bosque is a unique riparian area that extends for more than 100 miles along the central portion of the river through New Mexico, and is critical habitat along the central Rio Grande flyway, a major route for migrating birds. The Rio Grande and adjacent marshes provide food, water, and cover during the birds' long journey.

The nature center offers naturalist-led hikes, exhibits, teacher workshops, seasonal classes, and special events for visitors of all ages. The center also has a unique glass-walled library, which provides an opportunity to view birds and other wildlife in close proximity. A speaker system transmits outside sounds into the room.

Because this trail is obvious, specific Miles and Directions are not included here.

2 Piedras Marcadas Canyon

West of the city, the eastern edge of West Mesa exposes a 17-mile-long volcanic escarpment. A portion of the escarpment is protected in Petroglyph National Monument. This trail system leads hikers to the largest concentration of petroglyphs in the monument.

Distance: 1.8 miles out and back

Approximate hiking time: 1 hour

Difficulty: Easy

Trail surface: Dirt and rocks

Best season: Fall through spring

Water availability: None

Other trail users: None

Canine compatibility: Dogs on leashes allowed

Fees and permits: None

Maps: USGS: Los Griegos

Trail contacts: Petroglyph National Monument, 4735 Unser Blvd. NW, Albuquerque 87120; (505) 899-0205; www.nps.gov/petr

Special considerations: During the summer, hike early in the day and carry plenty of water.

Finding the trailhead: From the junction of I-40 and I-25, drive west 3.8 miles on I-40 to exit 155. Turn right onto Coors Boulevard NW, drive 6.0 miles north, and then turn left onto Paseo del Norte. Drive 1.3 miles, and then turn right onto Golf Course Road NW. After 0.6 mile, turn left onto Jill Patricia Street. The small trailhead parking area is just ahead on the right. GPS: UTM 13S 346464E 3895264N

The Hike

Petroglyph National Monument was established to protect an estimated 20,000 petroglyphs from the encroachment of suburban Albuquerque. Although not a wilderness experience, Piedras Marcadas Canyon is one of the least visited portions of the monument. The main trail heads west, then

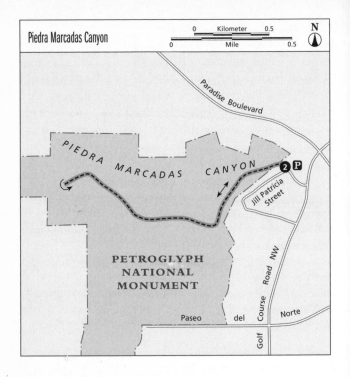

Piedra Marcadas Canyon

0   Kilometer   0.5

0   Mile   0.5

N

Paradise Boulevard

PIEDRA MARCADAS CANYON

2 P

Jill Patricia Street

PETROGLYPH
NATIONAL
MONUMENT

Golf Course Road NW

Paseo   del   Norte

southwest, and soon turns west into Piedras Marcadas Canyon. Along the way, several side loops lead to petroglyph areas. There are a large number of informal trails, but the area is small and it's difficult to get lost. Plans are afoot to close the informal trails to protect the resource.

Petroglyphs are rock carvings (as opposed to pictographs, which are rock paintings) created by chipping away the rock surface with stone tools. When the dark desert varnish is removed, the lighter rock underneath stands out. Most of the monument's petroglyphs were probably created by ancestors of the Pueblo Indians still living in the area. Pueblo

Indians have lived in the Rio Grande Valley since 500 A.D., but most of the artwork was done between 1300 and 1700. A few petroglyphs predate the Pueblo period and may be as old as 2,000 years. Others were carved by Spanish settlers in the 1700s.

Petroglyphs are fragile! Look, take photos, and make drawings, but don't touch the petroglyphs. Skin oil contaminates the rock surface and destroys the color of the artwork.

Because this trail is obvious, specific Miles and Directions are not provided here.

3 The Volcanoes

This trail loops past three volcanoes on the west side of the city, known locally as the Albuquerque Volcanoes or the Three Sisters. The area offers excellent views of the city and the Sandia Mountains to the east, as well as a close-up view of lava flows, cinder cones, and other volcanic features.

Distance: 3.0-mile loop with a short cherry stem section
Approximate hiking time: 2 hours
Difficulty: Easy
Trail surface: Dirt and rocks
Best season: Fall through spring
Water availability: None
Other trail users: None
Canine compatibility: Dogs on leashes allowed

Fees and permits: None
Maps: USGS: The Volcanoes
Trail contacts: Petroglyph National Monument, 4735 Unser Blvd. NW, Albuquerque 87120; (505) 899-0205; www.nps.gov/petr
Special considerations: During the summer, hike early in the day and carry plenty of water.

Finding the trailhead: From the junction of I-40 and I-25, drive west 9.5 miles to exit 149. Turn right onto Paseo del Vulcan and drive 4.9 miles north, then turn right onto an unsigned road and drive 0.3 mile to the trailhead. GPS: UTM 13S 337764E 3889016N

The Hike

From the trailhead, start off on the right-hand trail, heading southeast toward JA Volcano, the southernmost of the three volcanoes. The trail loops around the east side of JA and Black Volcanoes, and then heads north to Vulcan Volcano. After looping around Vulcan Volcano, the return trail heads southwest to the trailhead.

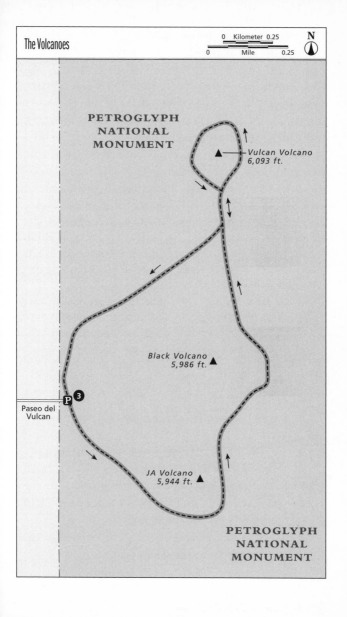

The Volcanoes

0   Kilometer   0.25

0   Mile   0.25

N

PETROGLYPH
NATIONAL
MONUMENT

Vulcan Volcano
6,093 ft.

Black Volcano
5,986 ft.

Paseo del
Vulcan

P 3

JA Volcano
5,944 ft.

PETROGLYPH
NATIONAL
MONUMENT

These three volcanoes are aligned north to south because they are part of a fissure eruption, where magma rises to the surface along cracks in the earth. In contrast, most volcanoes form around a single, central vent. This fissure is over 5 miles long. When active about 150,000 years ago, the volcanoes formed a "curtain of fire," much like that occurring today on the main island of Hawaii.

The fissure is part of the Rio Grande Rift Valley, which runs from southern Colorado to El Paso. It is one of only a few active rift valleys on the planet. In a rift zone, the crust of the earth is being stretched by mountain-building forces. Large blocks of crust drop down to form valleys, while blocks on the sides of the valleys rise. The cracks that open between blocks often provide paths for magma to rise to the surface and spread out into lava flows or erupt into fissure volcanoes.

Miles and Directions

- **0.0** Leave The Volcanoes Trailhead on the right-hand Volcanoes Trail.
- **0.5** Stay right at a trail junction to continue around the south side of JA Volcano.
- **1.2** Stay right at another trail junction and head north toward Vulcan Volcano.
- **1.5** Stay right at the junction with the return trail and walk the short cherry stem section.
- **1.7** Turn right onto the loop around Vulcan Volcano.
- **2.1** At the completion of the loop around Vulcan Volcano, stay right and rehike the short cherry stem section.
- **2.3** Turn right onto the return trail.
- **3.0** Arrive back at The Volcanoes Trailhead.

4 Jaral Cabin

This hike along the western foothills of the Sandia Mountains takes you to the ruins of an old ranger station, which harks back to the early days of the US Forest Service, when Albuquerque was still a distant city and rangers patrolled the forest backcountry on horseback. It's a good sunrise or sunset hike during the hot months and enjoyable any time of day the rest of the year.

Distance: 2.4 miles out and back

Approximate hiking time: 2 hours

Difficulty: Easy

Trail surface: Dirt and rocks

Best season: Fall through spring

Water availability: None

Other trail users: Equestrians

Canine compatibility: Dogs on leashes allowed

Fees and permits: Trailhead parking fee

Maps: USGS: Sandia Crest

Trail contacts: Cibola National Forest, 2113 Osuna Rd. NE, Albuquerque 87113; (505) 346-3900; www.fs.fed.us/r3/cibola/districts/sandia.shtml

Special considerations: During the summer, hike early or late in the day and carry plenty of water.

Finding the trailhead: From the junction of I-40 and I-25 in Albuquerque, drive 7.5 miles north on I-25 and take exit 234. Turn right onto NM 556 (Tramway Road NE), drive 5.1 miles, and turn left to remain on Tramway Road NE (NM 556 continues straight ahead). Drive 1.0 mile to the end of the road and park in the upper tramway parking lot. GPS: UTM 13S 365325E 3895331N

The Hike

This short but pleasant hike follows the Tramway Trail north from the trailhead. The trail skirts just east of private land; please obey signs and stay on the trail. Just after the Rozamiento Trail joins from the left, watch for the ruins of Jaral Cabin below the Tramway Trail to the west. The cabin was used as a ranger station and was probably built by the Civilian Conservation Corps sometime in the 1930s.

Small ranger stations such as Jaral Cabin were built all over the national forests in the first years of the US Forest Service to serve as bases for patrolling and working rangers. Before World War II, most travel through the rugged terrain of the national forests was by horseback or on foot, so rangers needed bases through the lands under their stewardship. The national forest reserves were established by an act of Congress in 1891 and later become the national forests. The US Forest Service was created in 1905 under the Department of Agriculture, primarily to administer the national forests. Some people express surprise that the Forest Service is under the Department of Agriculture rather than Interior, which oversees most of the other land management agencies such as the Bureau of Land Management and the National Park Service. The reason lies in the perpetual battle between traditional conservationists and preservationists. Conservationists want to protect the national lands from excessive exploitation but at the same time believe that all their resources should be utilized for the country as a whole. Preservationists, on the other hand, see the national lands as a resource to be protected in its natural state as much as possible. The first chief of the US Forest Service, Gifford Pinchot, was a classic conservationist, and his philosophy of forest management was later codified into law, directing the national forests to "produce the greatest good for the greatest number." The first director of the National Park Service, Stephen Mather, was an ardent preservationist, and

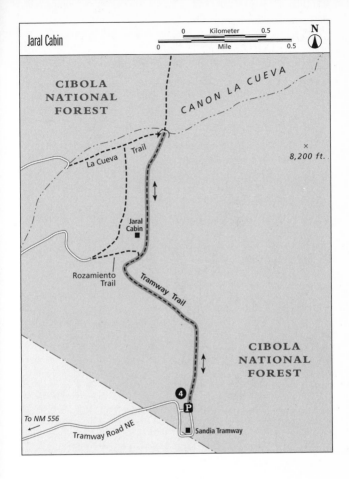

his philosophy that preserving the national parks for future generations to enjoy is still the guiding principle of the National Park Service.

Today, both management philosophies are under stress as a growing and more mobile population demands more from all the national lands.

Miles and Directions

0.0 Leave the Tramway Trailhead and hike north on the Tramway Trail.

0.7 Pass the junction with the Rozamiento Trail; stay right on the Tramway Trail.

0.8 The ruins of Jaral Cabin are visible below to the left.

1.2 Junction with the La Cueva Trail and end of the hike; return the way you came.

2.4 Arrive back at the Tramway Trailhead.

5 Embudito Trail

This trail climbs the western slopes of the Sandia Mountains to beautiful meadows on the Sandia Crest just south of South Sandia Peak. Although a longer climb than the east side trails that go to the beautiful South Sandia Peak area, the rugged canyons and rock formations of the western Sandia escarpment are worth the effort.

Distance: 9.4 miles out and back
Approximate hiking time: 7 hours
Difficulty: Moderate due to distance and elevation gain
Trail surface: Dirt and rocks
Best season: Fall through spring
Water availability: None
Other trail users: Equestrians
Canine compatibility: Dogs on leashes allowed
Fees and permits: Trailhead parking fee

Maps: USGS: Sandia Crest, Tijeras
Trail contacts: Cibola National Forest, 2113 Osuna Rd. NE, Albuquerque 87113; (505) 346-3900; www.fs.fed.us/r3/cibola/districts/sandia.shtml
Special considerations: During the summer, hike early or late in the day and carry plenty of water. The upper portions of the trail may be snow-covered during the winter and spring.

Finding the trailhead: From the junction of I-40 and I-25 in Albuquerque, drive 2.0 miles north on I-25, and take exit 228. Turn right onto Montgomery Boulevard and drive 7.0 miles. Turn left onto Glenwood Hills NE, drive 0.4 mile, and turn right into the Embudito Trailhead. GPS: UTM 13S 365007E 3889171N

The Hike

Initially, the Embudito Trail climbs east just above the bed of Embudito Canyon, gradually climbing higher above the bed. A steady climb leads to a shoulder, where the trail con-

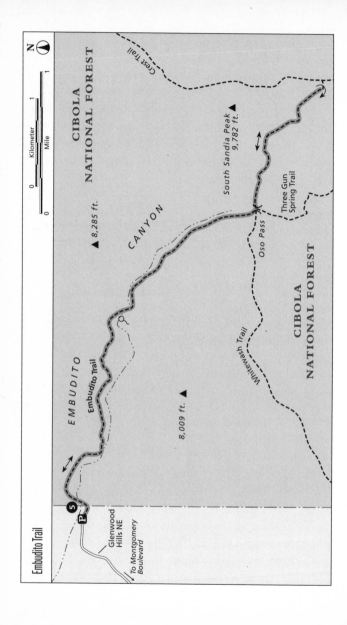

Embudito Trail

CIBOLA NATIONAL FOREST

Crest Trail

▲ 8,285 ft.

CANYON

EMBUDITO

Embudito Trail

South Sandia Peak
▲ 9,782 ft.

Three Gun
Spring Trail

Oso Pass

Whitewash Trail

▲ 8,009 ft.

CIBOLA
NATIONAL FOREST

P
5

Glenwood Hills NE

To Montgomery
Boulevard

N

0   Kilometer   1
0   Mile   1

tours, giving a break in the steady climb, to join the bed of Embudito Canyon at a seasonal spring. This fine spot makes a good turnaround point for those who wish to make this an easy hike.

The trail then follows Embudito Canyon to the southeast up north-facing, lush slopes to a four-way trail junction at Oso Pass. The Whitewash Trail comes up the ridge from the west, and the Three Gun Trail comes up the slopes from the south. Turn left to stay on the Embudito Trail and follow it east up the steep and rocky ridge west of South Sandia Peak. The trail skirts the southwest slopes before reaching the Sandia Crest about a mile south of South Sandia Peak. The fine meadows along the crest are the turnaround point for the hike. Embudito Trail ends at the Crest Trail 0.1 mile east.

The route the Embudito Trail takes up Embudito Canyon is a classic study in microclimates. Although elevation is the primary factor influencing where plant and animal communities are found in the mountains, aspect, or the direction the slopes face, is important also. South-facing slopes are drier and hotter than north-facing slopes at the same elevation. Also, valley and canyon bottoms tend to be cooler and moister than nearby slopes and ridges, because on calm, clear nights, cool air forms near the ground and moves downslope to collect in low-lying areas. Because of microclimates, the sections where the Embudito Trail is on the north side of the canyon, traversing south-facing slopes, have the most desert-like plant communities. When the trail crosses the bed and climbs along the north-facing slopes toward Oso Pass, the vegetation is much more green and lush. Microclimates can allow plants to grow as much as 2,000 feet below or above their normal elevations.

Miles and Directions

0.0 Leave the Embudito Trailhead and follow the Embudito Trail east.

2.1 The Embudito Trail descends to Embudito Canyon, which is the turnaround point for an easy hike.

3.5 Cross Oso Pass at the junction with the Three Gun and Whitewash Trails; turn left to stay on the Embudito Trail.

4.7 Arrive at the Sandia Crest; return the way you came.

9.4 Arrive back at the Embudito Trailhead.

6 Three Gun Spring Trail

The Three Gun Spring Trail offers a shorter way than the Embudo Trail (not to be confused with the Embudito Trail) to reach the scenic saddle at the head of Embudo Canyon, and also gives you a sweeping view of Tijeras Canyon and the southern Sandia Mountains and the western escarpment of the range.

Distance: 4.2 miles out and back
Approximate hiking time: 4 hours
Difficulty: Moderate due to elevation gain
Trail surface: Dirt and rocks
Best season: Fall through spring
Water availability: None
Other trail users: Equestrians
Canine compatibility: Dogs on leashes allowed

Fees and permits: Trailhead parking fee
Maps: USGS: Tijeras
Trail contacts: Cibola National Forest, 2113 Osuna Rd. NE, Albuquerque 87113; (505) 346-3900; www.fs.fed.us/r3/cibola/districts/sandia.shtml
Special considerations: During the summer, hike early or late in the day and carry plenty of water.

Finding the trailhead: From the junction of I-40 and I-25 in Albuquerque, drive east 9.5 miles on I-40 to exit 170. Turn left onto NM 333 (Historic Route 66), and drive 1.8 miles east. Turn left onto Monticello Drive, drive 0.6 mile, and turn left onto Alegre Road. Drive 0.1 mile, turn right onto Tres Pistolas Drive NE, and drive 0.3 mile to the Three Gun Spring Trailhead. GPS: UTM 13S 368333E 3882479N

The Hike

From the trailhead, the Three Gun Spring Trail climbs steadily north up into the mouth of a broad, unnamed can-

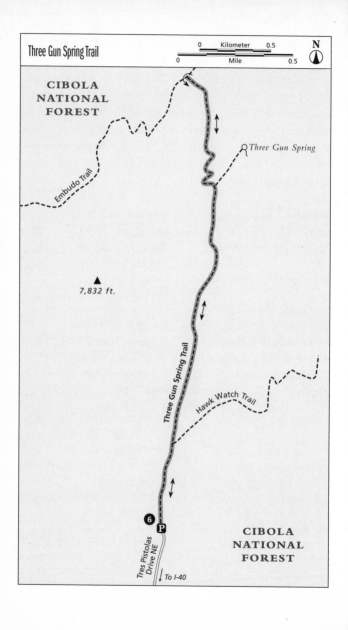

Three Gun Spring Trail

Kilometer

Mile

N

CIBOLA
NATIONAL
FOREST

Three Gun Spring

Embudo Trail

7,832 ft.

Three Gun Spring Trail

Hawk Watch Trail

6

P

Tres Pistolas Drive NE

To I-40

CIBOLA
NATIONAL
FOREST

yon. At the wilderness boundary, the Hawk Watch Trail forks right; stay left on the Three Gun Spring Trail, which continues north up a low ridge between two drainages. As the trail nears the head of the canyon, it drops into the drainage below Three Gun Spring. At the point where the main trail turns left and leaves the drainage, a spur trail forks right to Three Gun Spring. Stay left and follow the main Three Gun Spring Trail up the steep ascent to the junction with the Embudo Trail. This viewpoint is the end of the hike.

Supposedly, the Three Gun Spring and Trail got their names because three Spanish conquistador pistols were found in the area. There is no proof one way or the other, but it's intriguing to think of conquistadors in the area. Coronado's famous expedition came from Mexico City in search of gold and other wealth and spent 1540–1542 in the Albuquerque area. While there, Coronado sent out small exploring parties in several directions, always hoping to find wealth to plunder. His men were the first Europeans to visit both Kansas and the Grand Canyon, and they explored and mapped much of what is now New Mexico and eastern Arizona, but the expedition was deemed a failure. Privately financed at great expense by numerous investors, and even by some of the soldiers, a return on the investment was expected, and when Coronado returned to Mexico City empty-handed and in disgrace, the Spanish lost interest in their far northwestern American territories for half a century.

Miles and Directions

0.0 Leave the Three Gun Spring Trailhead and hike north on the Three Gun Spring Trail.

0.5 Cross the wilderness boundary at the junction with the Hawk Watch Trail; stay left on the Three Gun Spring Trail.

1.5 Pass the junction with the spur trail to Three Gun Spring; stay left on the main Three Gun Spring Trail.

2.1 Arrive at the junction with the Embudo Trail (not to be confused with the Embudito Trail); return the way you came.

4.2 Arrive back at the Three Gun Spring Trailhead.

Sandia Mountains

A lthough the Sandia Mountains are small, only 17 miles long and about 8 miles wide, the dramatic elevation range, from less than 6,000 feet at the foothills to 10,594 feet at Sandia Crest, the proximity to Albuquerque, and the ease of public access make the Sandias an extremely popular destination for hikers and other outdoor enthusiasts.

Geologically, the Sandia Mountains are a fault block range, in which large blocks of crust are uplifted to form long, narrow mountain ranges, and adjacent blocks are dropped down to form valleys. Part of the Rio Grande Rift System, the Sandias were formed about ten million years ago. The dominant bedrock is Sandia granite, a 1.5-billion-year-old metamorphic rock high in potassium feldspar, the mineral that gives Sandia granite its distinctly pinkish tint. Some much younger sedimentary rocks, mainly sandstone and limestone, cap parts of the range.

Four distinct life zones can be found as you ascend the slopes of the Sandias. Along the foothills, at about 6,000 feet, high desert grassland of the Upper Sonoran Life Zone dominates, but as you ascend, small juniper trees appear and soon become mixed with pinyon pines. At about 7,000 feet, ponderosa pine, the indicator tree of the Transition Life Zone, appears. At about 8,000 feet, other conifers such as Douglas fir begin to mix with the ponderosa, marking the Canadian Life Zone. Finally, above about 9,500 feet, the Hudsonian Life Zone appears, dominated by spruce and fir.

In contrast to the steep, rocky cliffs and escarpment of the western slope of the Sandia Mountains, the eastern slopes are gentle and heavily forested. These slopes make for a gentler hiking experience than the western escarpment, and some trails contour along the slopes with almost no elevation change. Others climb to the crest. Access to western slopes is via NM 14 and NM 536.

The northern end of the Sandia Mountains drops off suddenly to the broad, grassy savannas that separate the Sandias from the next range to the northeast, the southern end of the Sangre de Cristo Mountains. This gap also marks the transition from the Rocky Mountains to the Mexican Highlands, of which the Sandias are a part. The main access to the north end of the Sandias is NM 165.

7 Canoncito Trail

This hike follows the Canoncito Trail up the west slopes of the Sandias to the Sandia Crest and features small waterfalls and seasonal Canoncito Spring.

Distance: 6.8 miles out and back
Approximate hiking time: 5 hours
Difficulty: Moderate due to distance and elevation gain
Trail surface: Dirt and rocks
Best season: Spring through fall
Water availability: None
Other trail users: Equestrians
Canine compatibility: Dogs on leashes allowed

Fees and permits: Trailhead parking fee
Maps: USGS: Tijeras, Sandia Crest
Trail contacts: Cibola National Forest, 2113 Osuna Rd. NE, Albuquerque 87113; (505) 346-3900; www.fs.fed.us/r3/cibola/districts/sandia.shtml
Special considerations: Trails may be snow-covered during the winter and early spring.

Finding the trailhead: From the junction of I-40 and I-25 in Albuquerque, drive east 14.5 miles on I-40 to exit 175. Turn left onto NM 333, drive 0.8 mile, and then turn left onto NM 14. Drive 3.5 miles, and then turn left onto Canoncito Road and drive 0.5 mile to the locked gate. (The last portion of this road crosses private land. It is open to foot traffic but not vehicles.) GPS: UTM 13S 374654E 3888806N

The Hike

Walk up the road to the trailhead for Barts and Canoncito Trails, then take the Canoncito Trail to the right and follow it north. Go straight ahead where the Canoncito Trail crosses the Faulty Trail. The Canoncito Trail then climbs steadily west through the forest to end at the Sandia Crest

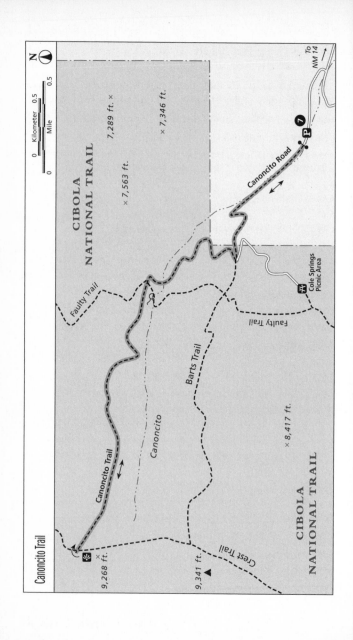

Canoncito Trail

CIBOLA NATIONAL TRAIL

CIBOLA NATIONAL TRAIL

Canoncito Trail

Faulty Trail

Canoncito

Barts Trail

Faulty Trail

Crest Trail

Canoncito Road

Cole Springs Picnic Area

To NM 14

P 7

× 7,289 ft.
× 7,346 ft.
× 7,563 ft.
× 8,417 ft.
× 9,268 ft.
▲ 9,341 ft.

N

0   Kilometer   0.5
0   Mile   0.5

and the Crest Trail. Walk south a few yards for a better view.

Ponderosa pines and tassel-eared squirrels are always found together. Agile climbers like most squirrels, the tassel-eared squirrels easily run up and down the rough-barked pines and among the branches and can leap up to 8 feet between branches. The squirrels are dependent on ponderosa pine for both nesting sites and food. They eat not only the seeds of the ponderosa pine but also the inner bark, flowers, and buds. They also eat fungi, carrion, and bones. Tassel-eared squirrels are also essential for the health of the pines, because they spread seeds and distribute spores from fungi that are symbiotic with the pines. They also bomb hikers and other intruders, running along the pine branches high above the trail and dropping green pine cones on the easy targets below.

Miles and Directions

0.0 Park at the locked gate and hike up the road.

0.9 Barts Trail and Canoncito Trail leave the road. Start up the Canoncito Trail on the right.

1.7 Cross the Faulty Trail and continue straight (west) on the Canoncito Trail.

3.4 Arrive at the Crest Trail and the Sandia Crest; return the way you came.

6.8 Arrive back at the parking area at the locked gate.

8 South Sandia Peak

This hike uses Barts Trail, an alternate way to reach the beautiful South Sandia Peak area along the Sandia Crest.

Distance: 8.4 miles out and back

Approximate hiking time: 8 hours

Difficulty: Moderate due to distance and elevation gain

Trail surface: Dirt and rocks

Best season: Spring through fall

Water availability: None

Other trail users: Equestrians

Canine compatibility: Dogs on leashes allowed

Fees and permits: Trailhead parking fee

Maps: USGS: Tijeras, Sandia Crest

Trail contacts: Cibola National Forest, 2113 Osuna Rd. NE, Albuquerque 87113; (505) 346-3900; www.fs.fed.us/r3/cibola/districts/sandia.shtml

Special considerations: Trails may be snow-covered during the winter and early spring.

Finding the trailhead: From the junction of I-40 and I-25 in Albuquerque, drive east 14.5 miles on I-40 to exit 175. Turn left onto NM 333, drive 0.8 mile, and then turn left onto NM 14. Drive 3.5 miles, and then turn left onto Canoncito Road and drive 0.5 mile to the locked gate. (The last portion of this road crosses private land. It is open to foot traffic but not vehicles.) GPS: UTM 13S 374654E 3888806N

The Hike

Walk up the road to the trailhead for Barts and Canoncito Trails, then take the Barts Trail up the slope to the west. Barts Trail crosses Faulty Trail, then climbs steadily to end at the Crest Trail. Turn left and follow the Crest Trail south along an especially scenic section, with views both east and

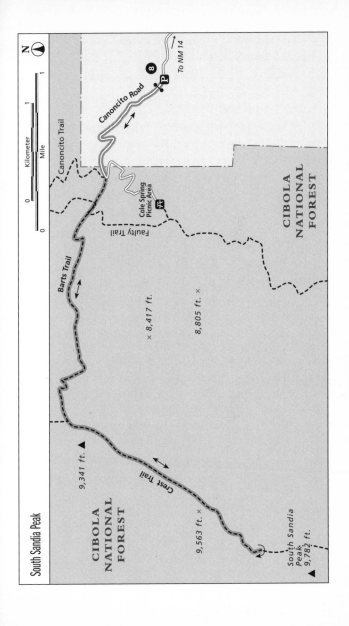

South Sandia Peak

CIBOLA NATIONAL FOREST

CIBOLA NATIONAL FOREST

Canoncito Trail

Canoncito Road

To NM 14

Cole Spring Picnic Area

Faulty Trail

Barts Trail

Crest Trail

9,341 ft. ▲

× 8,417 ft.

8,805 ft. ×

9,563 ft.

South Sandia Peak 9,782 ft. ▲

N

Kilometer

Mile

west. The saddle just north of South Sandia Peak where the Crest Trail leaves the crest is the turnaround point for this hike. Beyond this point, the Crest Trail skirts South Sandia Peak along its east slopes.

Barts Trail is named for local hiker Fayette "Bart" Barton, a Sandia enthusiast who constructed the original Barts Trail in 1979 with help from the New Mexico Mountain Club. The US Forest Service later rerouted portions of the trail and incorporated it into the official forest trail system.

Several species of yuccas grow in the pinyon-juniper woodland along the lower part of the trail. Banana yucca is especially common and can be identified by the long, stiff leaves growing from a common base. About 2 feet long, each slender leaf is marked by fibers curling off the edges and by a sharp spine at the tip. Like most yuccas, banana yuccas normally bloom during the spring by sending up a central bloom stalk, which reaches about 30 inches in height, topped by showy white blooms. Yuccas were an important food for natives.

Miles and Directions

0.0 Park at the locked gate and walk up the road.

0.9 The Barts Trail and the Canoncito Trail leave the road. Start up the Barts Trail, which is on the left.

1.0 Cross the Faulty Trail and continue west on the Barts Trail.

2.6 The Barts Trail ends at the Crest Trail; turn left onto the Crest Trail.

4.2 Arrive at the point where the Crest Trail leaves the crest at the saddle north of South Sandia Peak; return the way you came.

8.4 Arrive back at the parking area at the locked gate.

9 Cienega Trail

A pleasant and easier hike up a lush streambed to the Sandia Crest. *Cienega* is Spanish for "wet meadow," and you'll hike through several such lush meadows on this route.

Distance: 4.0 miles out and back

Approximate hiking time: 4 hours

Difficulty: Moderate due to elevation gain

Trail surface: Dirt and rocks

Best season: Spring through fall

Water availability: None

Other trail users: Equestrians

Canine compatibility: Dogs on leashes allowed

Fees and permits: Trailhead parking fee

Maps: USGS: Sandia Crest

Trail contacts: Cibola National Forest, 2113 Osuna Rd. NE, Albuquerque 87113; (505) 346-3900; www.fs.fed.us/r3/cibola/districts/sandia.shtml

Special considerations: Trails may be snow-covered during the winter and early spring.

Finding the trailhead: From the junction of I-40 and I-25 in Albuquerque, drive east 14.5 miles on I-40 to exit 175. Turn left onto NM 333, drive 0.8 mile, and then turn left onto NM 14. Drive 6.1 miles, and then turn left onto NM 536. Continue 1.8 miles, turn left onto the Sulphur Canyon Picnic Area Road, and turn left immediately. Drive 0.5 mile, turn right at a T intersection, and then drive another 0.5 mile through the Cienega Canyon Picnic Area to the trailhead at the end of the road. GPS: UTM 13S 373954E 3892730N

The Hike

From the trailhead, follow the Cienega Trail west up a pretty streambed. After crossing the Faulty Trail, the Cienega Trail continues west in a steady climb to a saddle on the

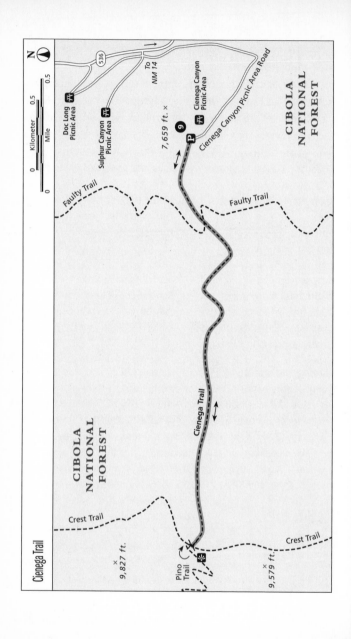

Cienega Trail

N

Doc Long
Picnic Area

Sulphur Canyon
Picnic Area

536

To
NM 14

7,659 ft. ×

Cienega Canyon
Picnic Area

9

P

Cienega Canyon Picnic Area Road

CIBOLA NATIONAL
FOREST

Faulty Trail

Faulty Trail

Kilometer   0.5

Mile   0.5

CIBOLA
NATIONAL
FOREST

Crest Trail

Cienega Trail

9,827 ft. ×

Pino
Trail

Crest Trail

9,579 ft. ×

Sandia Crest and the junctions of the Crest and Pino Trails. After enjoying the view, return the way you came.

Strictly speaking, *cienega* originated as a Spanish colonial name for a spring, but in modern use in the American Southwest, it refers to a wet, marshy area or meadow. Cienegas are fairly common in the Sandia Mountains and even more common in ranges with more rolling terrain. They are formed when groundwater comes to the surface in a fairly level area, which can be in a canyon bottom, a low area in a rolling, alpine grassland, or a meadow along a canyon bottom. Although cienegas are often associated with a stream, sometimes they are just a marshy area without flowing water. Needless to say, in the arid Southwest, cienegas are havens for wildlife and plant life, and often harbor rare or endangered species. Many cienegas throughout New Mexico have been lost to groundwater overpumping, diversion of streams and springs, pollution, and overgrazing, which makes the cienegas that are protected as part of the Sandia Mountain Wilderness all the more precious.

Miles and Directions

0.0 Leave the Cienega Trailhead and start on the Cienega Trail.

0.3 Cross the Faulty Trail and continue straight ahead on the Cienega Trail.

2.0 Arrive at the saddle on Sandia Crest; return the way you came.

4.0 Arrive back at the Cienega Trailhead.

10 Bill Spring–Sulphur Canyon Loop

Another pleasant hike on the lushly forested east slopes of the Sandias, this loop takes you through ponderosa pine and Gambel oak forest and past seasonal Wolf and Bill Springs.

Distance: 2.8-mile loop
Approximate hiking time: 2 hours
Difficulty: Easy
Trail surface: Dirt and rocks
Best season: Spring through fall
Water availability: None
Other trail users: Equestrians and mountain bikers
Canine compatibility: Dogs on leashes allowed

Fees and permits: Trailhead parking fee
Maps: USGS: Sandia Crest
Trail contacts: Cibola National Forest, 2113 Osuna Rd. NE, Albuquerque 87113; (505) 346-3900; www.fs.fed.us/r3/cibola/districts/sandia.shtml
Special considerations: Trails may be snow-covered during the winter and early spring.

Finding the trailhead: From the junction of I-40 and I-25 in Albuquerque, drive east 14.5 miles on I-40 to exit 175. Turn left onto NM 333, drive 0.8 mile, and then turn left onto NM 14. Drive 6.1 miles, and then turn left onto NM 536. Continue 1.8 miles, turn left onto the Sulphur Canyon Picnic Area Road, and drive to the picnic area and parking. GPS: UTM 13S 374189E 3893257N

The Hike

From the trailhead, the Sulphur Canyon Trail climbs west up Sulphur Canyon to end at the Faulty Trail and seasonal Wolf Spring. Turn right onto the Faulty Trail and follow it as it contours north through the dense forest. When the Faulty Trail meets the the Oso Corredor Trail junction, stay right and hike the Faulty Trail down into Tejano Canyon

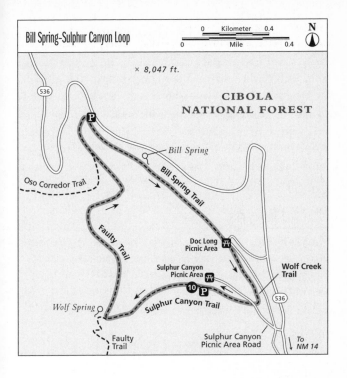

Bill Spring–Sulphur Canyon Loop

0 — Kilometer — 0.4
0 — Mile — 0.4

N

× 8,047 ft.

CIBOLA
NATIONAL FOREST

P

Bill Spring

Oso Corredor Trail

Bill Spring Trail

Faulty Trail

Doc Long
Picnic Area

Sulphur Canyon
Picnic Area

Wolf Creek
Trail

Wolf Spring

10 P

Sulphur Canyon Trail

536

Faulty
Trail

Sulphur Canyon
Picnic Area Road

To
NM 14

and Faulty Trailhead North. Turn right and follow the Bill
Spring Trail down the canyon to the southeast to Doc Long
Picnic Area. Now take the Wolf Creek Trail to the Sulphur
Canyon Picnic Area and the trailhead.

The Sulphur Canyon and Doc Long Picnic Areas were
built in the 1930s by the Civilian Conservation Corps,
commonly known as the CCC. One of many "alphabet
agencies" created by President Franklin Roosevelt and the
US Congress to provide employment during the depths of
the Great Depression, the CCC did a great deal of valu-
able conservation work on American public lands. The

CCC constructed hundreds of campgrounds and picnic areas throughout the national forests, as well as trails, roads, bridges, and other structures. Much of their work was of such high quality that it still endures today. Although the CCC was disbanded in 1942 as the federal focus shifted to the war effort, the CCC was the model for later federal and state corps programs such as the Student Conservation Association, the Environmental Corps, the California Conservation Corps, and many other successful organizations that are operating today.

Miles and Directions

0.0 Leave the Sulphur Canyon Trailhead at Sulphur Canyon Picnic Area and hike west on the Sulphur Canyon Trail.

0.4 End of the Sulphur Canyon Trail; turn right onto the Faulty Trail and pass the seasonal Wolf Spring.

1.1 Oso Corredor Trail comes in from the left; stay right on the Faulty Trail.

1.4 Pass Faulty Trailhead North and turn right onto the Bill Spring Trail.

2.1 Pass Doc Long Picnic Area and turn right onto the Wolf Creek Trail.

2.8 Arrive back at the Sulphur Canyon Trailhead.

11 Tree Spring Trail

This beautiful hike on the east slope of the Sandias takes you to the Sandia Crest south of the upper tram terminal. The upper portions of the trail pass through alpine fir and aspen forest, and wildflowers are common during spring and earlier summer. During the fall, the aspens shimmer with gold and yellow tones, streaking the mountainsides with color.

Distance: 3.8 miles out and back
Approximate hiking time: 3 hours
Difficulty: Easy
Trail surface: Dirt and rocks
Best season: Spring through fall
Water availability: None
Other trail users: Equestrians; mountain bikers outside the wilderness
Canine compatibility: Dogs on leashes allowed

Fees and permits: Trailhead parking fee
Maps: USGS: Sandia Crest
Trail contacts: Cibola National Forest, 2113 Osuna Rd. NE, Albuquerque 87113; (505) 346-3900; www.fs.fed.us/r3/cibola/districts/sandia.shtml
Special considerations: Trails may be snow-covered during the winter and early spring.

Finding the trailhead: From the junction of I-40 and I-25 in Albuquerque, drive east 14.5 miles on I-40 to exit 175. Turn left onto NM 333, drive 0.8 mile, and then turn left onto NM 14. Drive 6.1 miles, and then turn left onto NM 536. Continue 5.6 miles to the Tree Spring Trailhead on the left. GPS: UTM 13S 372116E 3895439N

The Hike

This popular trail climbs past the junction with the Oso Corredor Trail and continues up the heavily forested eastern slopes. One long switchback leads to the end of the trail at

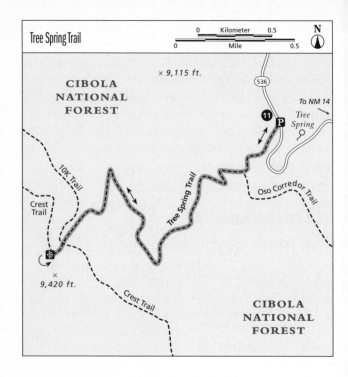

Kilometer

Mile

N

× 9,115 ft.

536

To NM 14

Tree
Spring

11 P

CIBOLA
NATIONAL
FOREST

10K Trail

Crest
Trail

Tree Spring Trail

Oso Corredor Trail

×
9,420 ft.

Crest Trail

CIBOLA
NATIONAL
FOREST

the Crest Trail junction. This is also the southern end of the
10K Trail. Turn left and follow the Crest Trail 0.1 mile west
to the Sandia Crest and a stunning view.

You'll see several different species of fir trees along this
hike, including Douglas fir, white fir, and corkbark fir. Of
the three, Douglas fir is not a true fir. True firs have cones
that stand upright on the branches, while the cones of
Douglas fir hang down. While both spruces and firs have
short needles that grow singly from the branches, they are
easy to tell apart. Fir needles are flat in cross section, while
spruce needles are square, so all you have to do is break off

a needle and try to roll it between your fingers. If it rolls, it's a spruce, and if not, it's a fir. There's only one pine with single needles—the singleleaf pinyon—and it grows at lower elevations than the firs and spruces.

White and Douglas firs can be a little harder to differentiate if there are no cones present. White fir is more of a bluish-green in color, compared to the deeper green of the Douglas fir. When they occur together, the difference is obvious. Also, Douglas fir is more common. Corkbark fir is easy to spot because the bark is silvery, soft, and corklike.

Miles and Directions

0.0 Leave the Tree Spring Trailhead and start on the Tree Spring Trail.

0.3 Oso Corredor Trail comes in from the left; continue straight on the Tree Spring Trail.

1.8 Tree Spring Trail ends at the 10K and Crest Trails; turn left onto the Crest Trail.

1.9 Arrive at the Sandia Crest and the viewpoint; return the way you came.

3.8 Arrive back at the Tree Spring Trailhead.

12 Osha Loop Trail

This longer hike near the Sandia Crest takes you along the upper east slopes of the Sandias on the 10K Trail, and then around the Osha Loop Trail north of Media Canyon. Aspens and the alpine fir forest are one of the attractions, as is the fall color.

Distance: 6.8 miles out and back with a loop at the end

Approximate hiking time: 4 hours

Difficulty: Easy

Trail surface: Dirt and rocks

Best season: Spring through fall

Water availability: None

Other trail users: Equestrians

Canine compatibility: Dogs on leashes allowed

Fees and permits: Trailhead parking fee

Maps: USGS: Sandia Crest

Trail contacts: Cibola National Forest, 2113 Osuna Rd. NE, Albuquerque 87113; (505) 346-3900; www.fs.fed.us/r3/cibola/districts/sandia.shtml

Special considerations: Trails may be snow-covered during the winter and early spring.

Finding the trailhead: From the junction of I-40 and I-25 in Albuquerque, drive east 14.5 miles on I-40 to exit 175. Turn left onto NM 333, drive 0.8 mile, and then turn left onto NM 14. Drive 6.1 miles, and then turn left onto NM 536. Continue 11.3 miles and park at the 10K Trailhead on the right side of the road. GPS: UTM 13S 368837E 3897173N

The Hike

Start on the 10K Trail and hike north to the Osha Loop Trail. Turn right and follow the Osha Loop Trail as it descends gradually northeast above Canon Media. There are occasional views of the canyon below, and then the trail turns north, passing the Osha Spring Trail. Stay left on the Osha Loop Trail, which now turns northwest and begins a gradual climb through the forest. After crossing the Ellis Trail, the Osha Loop Trail ends at the Crest Trail; turn left on the Crest Trail and hike a short distance to Del Agua overlook. Turn left onto the 10K Trail, which soon crosses the Survey and Ellis Trails; stay on the 10K Trail to return to the trailhead.

Quaking aspen is the most widespread tree in North America. It grows at the higher elevations in the New Mexico mountains, favoring cooler, north-facing slopes as well as sheltered canyon bottoms. The tall, graceful trees are up to 1 foot in diameter and reach about 50 to 70 feet in height. The smooth, white bark makes a vivid contrast to the associated evergreen trees. The leaves, which are attached by thin, flexible stems, shimmer in the slightest breeze. During the fall, the deciduous leaves turn brilliant shades of yellow, orange, and red, often slashing entire mountainsides with color. Aspens propagate via their root system, so that many hundreds of trees forming a stand are actually the same plant. They are often the first tree to grow back after a forest fire, because young aspens can tolerate open sunlight better than most evergreen seedlings. Quaking aspen only lives about one hundred years, but the aspen groves provide shade for the longer-lived firs and spruces to get a start. By the time the aspens are reaching old age, the evergreen trees are already replacing them.

In many areas, aspen groves harbor arborglyphs, or historic tree carvings. Mostly done by sheepherders of Basque ancestry, many of the carvings date back fifty years or more. Subjects range from simple lists of names to detailed depictions of people, wildlife, and buildings. Aspen bark is soft

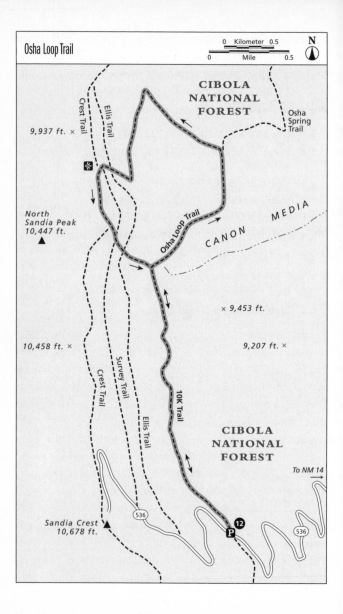

Osha Loop Trail

0   Kilometer   0.5

0   Mile   0.5

N

CIBOLA
NATIONAL
FOREST

Osha
Spring
Trail

9,937 ft. ×

Crest Trail

Ellis Trail

North
Sandia Peak
10,447 ft. ▲

Osha Loop Trail

CAÑON

MEDIA

× 9,453 ft.

10,458 ft. ×

9,207 ft. ×

Crest Trail

Survey Trail

Ellis Trail

10K Trail

CIBOLA
NATIONAL
FOREST

To NM 14

Sandia Crest
10,678 ft. ▲

536

12
P

536

and easy to carve, but don't be tempted yourself. Old aspen carvings are historic artifacts protected by law, but there are far too many of us now to indulge in tree carving.

Miles and Directions

0.0 Leave the 10K Trailhead and hike north on the 10K Trail.

1.9 Reach the junction with the Osha Loop Trail; turn right onto the Osha Loop Trail.

2.8 Pass the Osha Spring Trail junction and stay left on the Osha Loop Trail.

4.1 Cross the Ellis Trail and remain on the Osha Loop Trail.

4.3 Osha Loop Trail ends; turn left onto the Crest Trail.

4.5 Turn left onto the 10K Trail.

4.8 Cross the Ellis Trail and remain on the 10K Trail.

5.0 Osha Loop Trail goes left; stay on the 10K Trail.

6.8 Arrive back at the 10K Trailhead.

13 Crest Loop South

This scenic loop starts from Sandia Crest and loops below the crest for some dramatic views, then returns through the cool, shady, alpine aspen and fir forest on the crest. This is another great hike for fall color.

Distance: 3.1-mile loop
Approximate hiking time: 2 hours
Difficulty: Easy
Trail surface: Dirt and rocks
Best season: Spring through fall
Water availability: None
Other trail users: Equestrians on the Crest Trail portion
Canine compatibility: Dogs on leashes allowed

Fees and permits: Trailhead parking fee
Maps: USGS: Sandia Crest
Trail contacts: Cibola National Forest, 2113 Osuna Rd. NE, Albuquerque 87113; (505) 346-3900; www.fs.fed.us/r3/cibola/districts/sandia.shtml
Special considerations: Trails may be snow-covered during the winter and early spring.

Finding the trailhead: From the junction of I-40 and I-25 in Albuquerque, drive east 14.5 miles on I-40 to exit 175. Turn left onto NM 333, drive 0.8 mile, and then turn left onto NM 14. Drive 6.1 miles, and then turn left onto NM 536. Continue 13.4 miles to the end of the road, and park in the main parking lot. GPS: UTM 13S 368087E 3897439N

The Hike

Start on the Crest Spur Trail, which drops off the ridgeline to the south. The trail then descends gradually to end where it meets the La Luz Trail in a saddle. Turn left and follow the La Luz Trail as it contours south and east to meet the Crest Trail just north of the upper tram terminal. Turn left

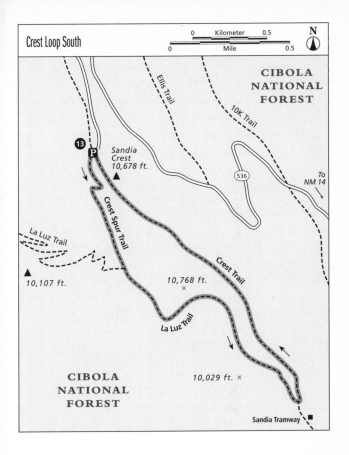

onto the Crest Trail and follow it back to the northwest along the crest through Kiwanis Meadow. After passing Sandia Crest with its crown of radio towers, the Crest Trail returns to the Sandia Crest Trailhead.

The Sandia Peak Tramway, whose upper terminal is at the south end of this loop hike, is the longest aerial tram in the world, spanning 2.7 miles and rising 4,000 feet. It serves

as both a scenic tram and a fast way to reach the top of the
Sandia Peak Ski Area, taking just fifteen minutes for the trip.
It was constructed by a Swiss engineering company, took
two years to build, and was completed in 1966. Construc-
tion was complicated by the difficult, rocky terrain, and the
cable alone took five months to lay. Even the Swiss experts
admitted that the Sandia Peak Tram was the hardest of the
more than fifty aerial trams they'd previously constructed.

Miles and Directions

0.0   Leave the Sandia Crest Trailhead and start on the Crest Spur
Trail.

0.6   The Crest Spur Trail ends at the La Luz Trail; turn left onto
the La Luz Trail.

1.8   Meet the Crest Trail at the upper tram terminal; turn left onto
the Crest Trail.

3.1   Arrive back at the Sandia Crest Trailhead.

14 Sandia Crest

This pleasant walk follows the Crest Trail along the Sandia Crest through cool alpine, fir, and aspen forest. It is one of the easiest ways to hike through fall color in the Sandias while enjoying the 100-mile views from the crest.

Distance: 4.2 miles out and back
Approximate hiking time: 2 hours
Difficulty: Easy
Trail surface: Dirt and rocks
Best season: Spring through fall
Water availability: None
Other trail users: Equestrians
Canine compatibility: Dogs on leashes allowed

Fees and permits: Trailhead parking fee
Maps: USGS: Sandia Crest
Trail contacts: Cibola National Forest, 2113 Osuna Rd. NE, Albuquerque 87113; (505) 346-3900; www.fs.fed.us/r3/cibola/districts/sandia.shtml
Special considerations: Trails may be snow-covered during the winter and early spring.

Finding the trailhead: From the junction of I-40 and I-25 in Albu-querque, drive east 14.5 miles on I-40 to exit 175. Turn left onto NM 333, drive 0.8 mile, and then turn left onto NM 14. Drive 6.1 miles, and then turn left onto NM 536. Continue 13.4 miles to the end of the road and park in the main parking lot. GPS: UTM 13S 368087E 3897439N

The Hike

Follow the Crest Trail north from the trailhead. The trail skirts the radio tower complex on the east, then joins the crest to start a steady descent. Several meadows and open-ings give views of the large rock formations along the west-ern escarpment of the Sandias.

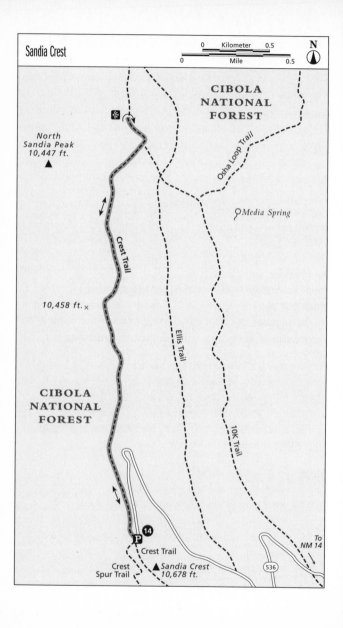

Sandia Crest

0   Kilometer   0.5

0   Mile   0.5

N

CIBOLA
NATIONAL
FOREST

North
Sandia Peak
10,447 ft.
▲

Osha Loop Trail

Media Spring

Crest Trail

10,458 ft. ×

Ellis Trail

CIBOLA
NATIONAL
FOREST

10K Trail

To
NM 14

P 14

Crest Trail

536

Crest
Spur Trail

▲ Sandia Crest
10,678 ft.

The Crest Trail leaves the crest south of North Sandia Peak and descends more steeply to the 10K Trail junction. Stay left on the Crest Trail and follow it a short distance to Del Agua overlook, another stunning viewpoint that is the turnaround point for the hike.

As you hike through the beautiful mixed forest of the Hudsonian Life Zone on this hike, you'll encounter two common spruce trees. The more common is Englemann spruce, which tolerates adverse conditions better than Colorado blue spruce. Englemann spruce grows right up to the tree line in the higher mountains to the north of the Sandias, while Colorado blue spruce favors more protected locations such as north slopes and drainages. The two spruces can be hard to tell apart, though the needles of the Colorado blue spruce are sharper and the cones tend to be a reddish-purple.

In exposed locations and near timberline, Englemann spruce can be found growing in low, ground-hugging mats and weird shapes known as "krummholz." Exposure to strong, freezing winds causes any exposed portion of the tree to die back, so that only those parts of the tree protected by snow drifts or boulders survive. This continual natural pruning results in a low-growing, dense mass of foliage that hugs the protecting object.

Miles and Directions

0.0 Leave the Sandia Crest Trailhead and hike north on the Crest Trail.

2.0 Pass the junction with the 10 K Trail and stay left on the Crest Trail.

2.1 Arrive at the Del Agua overlook; return the way you came.

4.2 Arrive back at the Sandia Crest Trailhead.

15 Crest Trail North

This hike starts at the north end of the Crest Trail and follows it to a viewpoint on the north end of the Sandia Crest. Although the trail climbs steadily, the views of the rugged canyons at the north end of the Sandia Mountains are worth the effort.

Distance: 6.6 miles out and back

Approximate hiking time: 4 hours

Difficulty: Moderate due to distance and elevation gain

Trail surface: Dirt and rocks

Best season: Spring through fall

Water availability: None

Other trail users: Equestrians

Canine compatibility: Dogs on leashes allowed

Fees and permits: Trailhead parking fee

Maps: USGS: Placitas

Trail contacts: Cibola National Forest, 2113 Osuna Rd. NE, Albuquerque 87113; (505) 346-3900; www.fs.fed.us/r3/cibola/districts/sandia.shtml

Special considerations: Trails may be snow-covered during the winter and early spring.

Finding the trailhead: From the junction of I-40 and I-25 in Albuquerque, drive 15.8 miles north onto I-25 exit 242. Turn right onto NM 165 and drive 5.1 miles. Turn right onto Tunnel Spring Road and drive 1.5 miles to the Tunnel Spring Trailhead. GPS: UTM 13S 369108E 3906317N

The Hike

At its northern end, the Crest Trail uses a circuitous route to climb the steep northern end of the Sandia Crest while keeping a moderate grade. From the Tunnel Spring Trailhead, the Crest Trail heads east, soon passing the wilderness boundary, and heads several drainages before turning

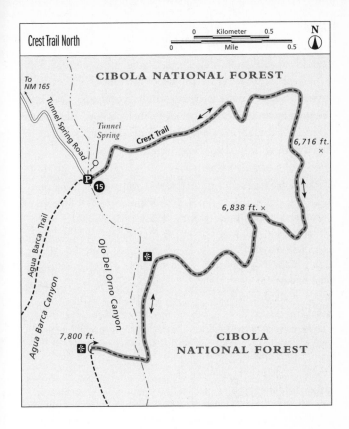

CIBOLA NATIONAL FOREST

To NM 165

Tunnel Spring Road

Tunnel Spring

Crest Trail

6,716 ft.

6,838 ft.

P 15

Agua Barca Trail

Ojo Del Orno Canyon

Agua Barca Canyon

7,800 ft.

CIBOLA NATIONAL FOREST

abruptly south. Here the trail climbs above a ravine to reach somewhat gentler slopes above, where it turns west and climbs via several broad switchbacks. The Crest Trail first reaches the steeply descending Sandia Crest above Ojo del Orno Canyon, where there are great views. Hikers wishing a shorter hike can turn around here. Otherwise, continue as the Crest Trail turns south to cross the head of Ojo del Orno Canyon. After crossing the drainage, the Crest Trail turns west again and climbs to an even more spectacular viewpoint above Agua Barca Canyon. This is the turn-around point for the hike.

Along this hike, you'll see Colorado pinyon pines mixed in with juniper trees, forming a low woodland. Colorado pinyons have two short needles per bunch and reach about 10 to 20 feet high. The seeds from the cones, known as pine nuts, were an important food source for natives and settlers alike and are still popular today.

Found living among the pinyons and completely dependent on them for survival is the pinyon jay. This large songbird is a dull blue in color, except for a paler chin, and travels in large flocks. Its distinctive, nasal caw is a classic sound throughout the pinyon-juniper woodlands of the West. Although pinyon jays are omnivorous, they mainly eat pinyon pine nuts, which they cache during the late summer and fall against the lean times of winter and spring. Pinyon jays have incredible spatial memories and can find more than 90 percent of their nut caches, even under several inches of snow.

Miles and Directions

0.0 Leave the Tunnel Spring Trailhead and follow the Crest Trail.

1.1 The Crest Trail turns south.

1.7 The Crest Trail turns west.

2.5 Cross Ojo del Orno Canyon on the Crest Trail.

3.3 Arrive at the viewpoint overlooking Agua Barca Canyon; return the way you came.

6.6 Arrive back at Tunnel Spring Trailhead.

16 Sandia Cave

A short walk to a cave containing one of the most important archaeological sites in North America. Controversy swirls around the ages of some of the artifacts, which may be as old as 35,000 years.

Distance: 1.0 mile out and back
Approximate hiking time: 1 hour
Difficulty: Easy
Trail surface: Dirt and rocks
Best season: Spring through fall
Water availability: None
Other trail users: None
Canine compatibility: Dogs are not allowed
Fees and permits: Trailhead parking fee
Maps: USGS: Placitas
Trail contacts: Cibola National Forest, 2113 Osuna Rd. NE, Albuquerque 87113; (505) 346-3900; www.fs.fed.us/r3/cibola/districts/sandia.shtml
Special considerations: Trails may be snow-covered during the winter and early spring.

Finding the trailhead: From the junction of I-40 and I-25 in Albuquerque, drive 18.5 miles north on I-25 to exit 242. Turn right onto NM 165 and drive 11.7 miles to the Sandia Cave Trailhead. The last portion of this road is dirt. GPS: UTM 13S 371748E 3901707N

The Hike

From the trailhead, the Sandia Cave Trail climbs slightly as it traverses along the east wall of Las Huertas Canyon to reach the cave. Sandia Cave was first excavated in 1935, and artifacts were soon discovered that clearly belonged to the Folsom Culture, about 10,000 to 12,000 years ago. The Folsom Culture was already known from other sites, but shortly afterward, a young archaeologist, Frank Hibben, made an astounding discovery of artifacts from a much

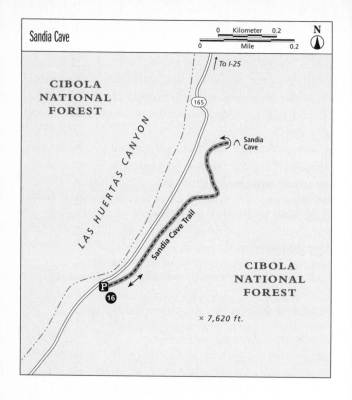

Sandia Cave

0　　Kilometer　0.2
0　　Mile　　　0.2

N

CIBOLA
NATIONAL
FOREST

To I-25

(165)

Sandia
Cave

LAS HUERTAS CANYON

Sandia Cave Trail

P
16

CIBOLA
NATIONAL
FOREST

× 7,620 ft.

earlier culture. Radio carbon dating seemed to prove that these people used Sandia Cave 25,000 to 35,000 years ago. This was evidence of man in North America far earlier than had been thought.

Pueblo peoples have lived in and around the Sandia Mountains for thousands of years. Pueblo groups are distinguished from other native groups by many factors, but the one that gives the Puebloans their name is their style of dwelling: adobe and stonework buildings organized into small towns, often defensive by design. The modern native peoples are believed to have descended from the Anasazi, a culture that constructed large pueblos and cliff dwellings in the Four Corners region. Other groups that may be ancestors of the New Mexico Pueblo people are the Hohokam, a culture that reached its maximum in central Arizona, and the Mogollon culture, which thrived in and around the Mogollon Mountains in west-central New Mexico.

Pueblos near Albuquerque include Isleta Pueblo to the south, Laguna Pueblo to the west, and Sandia, Santa Ana, Zia, Jemez, San Felipe, Santa Domingo, and Cochiti Pueblos to the north.

Miles and Directions

0.0 Leave the Sandia Cave Trailhead and hike north on the Sandia Cave Trail.

0.5 Arrive at Sandia Cave; return the way you came.

1.0 Arrive back at the Sandia Cave Trailhead.

Other Areas

T he countryside to the north of Albuquerque has limited public access due to private land and pueblos. This section includes a couple of hikes in a new historic park and a new national monument, as well as a backdoor route into Bandelier National Monument and a sample hike in the Manzano Mountains southeast of the city.

The Manzano Mountains are named for apple orchards planted in a nearby town; *manzano* means "apple tree" in Spanish. The range is about 25 miles southeast of Albuquerque, and elevations range as high as 10,098 feet at Manzano Peak. There are several other prominent summits, including Bosque Peak (9,610 feet), Mosca Peak (9,509 feet), and Guadalupe Peak (9,450 feet). Bosque and Guadalupe Peak are prominent pyramidal peaks as seen from Albuquerque.

Geologically, this small range is an extension of the Sandia Mountains, and together the two ranges are considered to be the northern end of the Mexican Highlands geologic province. The Manzanos are separated from the Sandias by Tijeras Canyon, the route of I-40. The Manzano Mountains are part of the same fault block that created the Sandias, but the range is gentler in relief, lacking the dramatic eastern escarpment and cliffs of the Sandias.

Plant and animal life are similar to the Sandia Mountains and encompass the same four life zones: the Upper Sonoran,

Transition, Canadian, and Hudsonian Zones. Vegetation ranges from high-desert savanna along the 6,000-foot base of the mountain to pinyon pine–juniper woodland in the foothills up to about 7,000 feet; ponderosa pine, from about 7,000 feet to 9,000 feet; and finally Douglas fir, Englemann spruce, and quaking aspen along the highest ridges and on the north-facing slopes.

Although the northern foothills are adjacent to the city and much of the range is in the Cibola National Forest, public access is limited because of Kirtland Air Force Base and Isleta Pueblo to the north and private land to the west. Primary public access is from the east side, via NM 337 and NM 55. Because of the limited access, the Manzanos are much less visited than the Sandia Mountains.

17 Cerrillos Hills Historic Park

A hike through rolling desert terrain through a historic mining area. Lying at lower elevations than many of the hikes, this area is enjoyable year-round. Numerous mine shafts, workings, and other remnants of the mining period are found along the trails.

Distance: 4.3-mile loop
Approximate hiking time: 3 hours
Difficulty: Easy
Trail surface: Dirt and rocks
Best season: Fall through spring
Water availability: None
Other trail users: Equestrians and mountain bikers
Canine compatibility: Dogs on leashes allowed
Fees and permits: None

Maps: USGS: Picture Rock, Madrid
Trail contacts: Santa Fe County Open Space and Trail Program, P.O. Box 276, Santa Fe, NM 87504-0276; (505) 992-9868; www.co.santa-fe.nm.us/resident/open_space_trails.php
Special considerations: During the summer, hike early or late in the day and carry plenty of water.

Finding the trailhead: From the junction of I-40 and I-25 in Albuquerque, drive 41.0 miles north on I-25 to exit 267. Turn right onto CR 57, drive 8.0 miles, and then turn left onto CR 57A. Drive 0.7 mile to the parking lot at Cerrillos Hills Historic Park. GPS: UTM 13S 398116E 3922970N

The Hike

From the trailhead, cross the road to the east and start up the Jane Calvin Sanchez Trail, which swings north around a ridge, then follows a drainage up to the first of several old mines. After passing a second old mine, you'll reach a third mine at a trail junction; turn left here to stay on the Jane Calvin Sanchez Trail. The trail descends back to the main road, Camino Turquesa at Mineral Spring.

Turn left onto the main road, walk a few yards, and pick up the Escalante Trail on the west side of the road. This trail climbs west, and then turns north. You'll pass the Elkins Canyon, Cortez Mine, and Coyote Trails in quick succession; at each junction, continue straight on the Escalante Trail. The Escalante Trail ends at a private land boundary; turn left onto the Mirador Trail, which heads southwest. A short spur trail leads right 0.1 mile to the Mirador Viewpoint; after taking in the view, return to the main Mirador Trail and turn right to continue the loop.

When the Mirador Trail ends at the Coyote Trail, turn right and follow the Coyote Trail southwest along the slope below a ridge. The Coyote Trail abruptly turns east and ends at the Elkins Canyon Trail. Turn right onto the Elkins Canyon Trail and follow it generally south until it descends southeast to meet a road. Turn left on the road, and then, just before the road joins the main park road, Camino Turquesa, turn left onto an unnamed trail that closely parallels Camino Turquesa, and follow this trail north to the trailhead.

The mining history of the Cerrillos Hills goes back well before Europeans arrived in the area. Pottery shards in the area date back to around 900 A.D., most of which came from the nearby San Marcos Pueblo, which was a major center of pottery making in the middle Rio Grande Valley. The Cerrillos Hills are the origin of much of the lead used to make glaze paint by potters living along the Rio Grand between about 1300 and 1700 A.D. Numerous archaeological sites in the Cerrillos Hills attest to Puebloan mining and

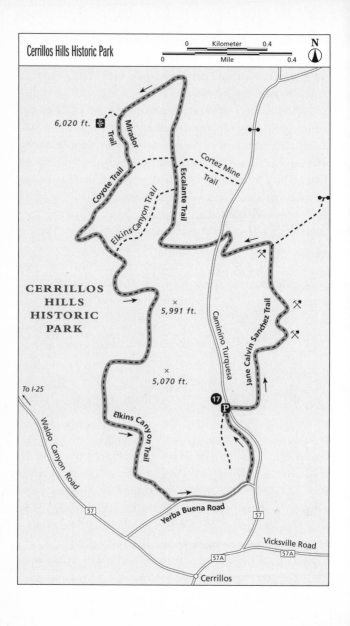

Cerrillos Hills Historic Park

Kilometer
0   0.4

Mile
0   0.4

N

6,020 ft.

Mirador Trail

Coyote Trail

Cortez Mine Trail

Escalante Trail

Elkins Canyon Trail

CERRILLOS
HILLS
HISTORIC
PARK

× 5,991 ft.

Camino Turquesa

Jane Calvin Sanchez Trail

× 5,070 ft.

To I-25

17 P

Elkins Canyon Trail

Waldo Canyon Road

57

Yerba Buena Road

57

Vicksville Road

57A   57A

Cerrillos

related activities, including galena mines, quarries, refining areas, shard areas, campsites, fireplaces, and workshops. It's possible that the Mina del Tiro is one of the oldest galena mines in the New World.

In 1879 a mining boom resulted in an influx of miners and prospectors, who quickly established more than 1,000 claims. Several boom towns sprang up to service the mines, but only one, Cerrillos, survives today, its survival assured by the arrival of the railroad in 1880. A few mines were worked into the twentieth century, but the Great Depression was the end of serious mining in the Cerrillos Hills. In the 1970s an attempt to open a large-scale copper mine was made, but local opposition and environmental questions, including concern about groundwater pollution, along with the falling price of copper, soon scuttled the project.

Miles and Directions

0.0 Leave the trailhead and cross the road to start on the Jane Calvin Sanchez Trail.

0.7 A spur trail goes right; stay left on the Jane Calvin Sanchez Trail.

0.9 Cross Camino Turquesa, then turn left and walk a few yards along the road, and then turn right onto the Escalante Trail.

1.3 Pass the Elkins Canyon Trail on the left; continue straight ahead on the Escalante Trail.

1.4 Pass the Cortez Mine Trail on the right and the Coyote Trail on the left; continue straight ahead on the Escalante Trail.

1.6 Turn left onto the Mirador Trail at a private property boundary.

1.9 Turn right onto a side trail to the Mirador Viewpoint.

2.0 Arrive at Mirador Viewpoint; retrace your steps to the main Mirador Trail.

2.1 Back at the main Mirador Trail, turn right to continue the loop.

2.3 The Mirador Trail ends; turn right onto the Coyote Trail.

2.7 Now, the Coyote Trail ends at Elkins Canyon Trail; turn right.

3.8 The Elkins Canyon Trail ends at Yerba Buena Road; turn left and follow this road.

4.1 Leave the road for an unnamed trail on the left that closely parallels Camino Turquesa.

4.3 Arrive back at the trailhead.

18 Canyon Trail

This hike follows a national recreation trail at Kasha–Katuwe Tent Rocks National Monument through unusual geologic formations and a narrow canyon to a viewpoint overlooking the Tent Rocks.

Distance: 3.3-mile loop and cherry stem
Approximate hiking time: 2 hours
Difficulty: Easy
Trail surface: Dirt and rocks
Best season: Fall through spring
Water availability: None
Other trail users: None
Canine compatibility: Dogs on leashes allowed
Fees and permits: Entrance fee
Maps: USGS: Canada
Trail contacts: Bureau of Land Management, Rio Puerco Field Office, 435 Montano NE, Albuquerque 87107; (505) 761-8700; www.blm.gov/nm/st/en/prog/recreation/rio_puerco/kasha_katuwe_tent_rocks.html
Special considerations: During the summer, hike early or late in the day and carry plenty of water. During rainy weather or when there is a threat of thunderstorms and flash flooding, do not hike the Canyon Trail.

Finding the trailhead: From the junction of I-40 and I-25 in Albuquerque, drive 32.9 miles north onto exit 267. Turn left onto NM 22 o I-25 and drive 12.3 miles. Turn left to remain on NM 22 (IR 90 continues straight head). Drive 1.7 miles, and then turn right onto IR 92 and drive 4.8 miles, past the fee station, to the parking area. GPS: UTM 13S 372238E 3946868N

The Hike

From the trailhead, start hiking on the right fork of the Cave Loop Trail. This trail climbs gradually northeast up a broad valley, crosses a drainage, and then nears the steep eastern slopes. Leave the Cave Loop Trail here and turn right onto the Canyon Trail, which heads north up a narrow canyon. Toward its end, this canyon turns sharply left (west), and the trail climbs the head of the canyon. After turning south, the Canyon Trail ends at a viewpoint overlooking the Tent Rocks and views of the distant Sangre de Cristo, Jemez, and Sandia Mountains, as well as the Rio Grande Valley.

After enjoying the view, retrace your steps to the Cave Loop Trail, and then turn right. The Cave Loop Trail skirts the base of the steep slopes, passes a cave, then turns south along the base of the Tent Rocks to return to the trailhead.

Kasha-Katuwe means "white cliffs" in the traditional language of Cochiti Pueblo.

Volcanic eruptions occurring about seven million years ago are responsible for the cone-shaped Tent Rocks. Huge explosions created pyroclastic flows of searing hot gases and ash, which roared down slopes, while glassy rock fragments rained down from above. A thousand feet of volcanic ash, pumice, and tuff were deposited in the Tent Rocks area. Erosion, primarily by water, later exposed these soft deposits, now called the Peralta tuff, and carved them into their present shapes. Hard cap rocks, part of the overlying Cochiti formation, protected the softer rock below as the terrain eroded, and the result is the distinctive cone shapes. Once the cap rock disappears, the cone erodes away completely. Cones from a few feet to 90 feet high can be seen in the national monument, some with and some without their protective cap stones.

Apache tears, which are small, teardrop-shaped pieces of obsidian, or volcanic glass, are found in the drainages. These hard bits of black, natural glass are similar to man-made glass

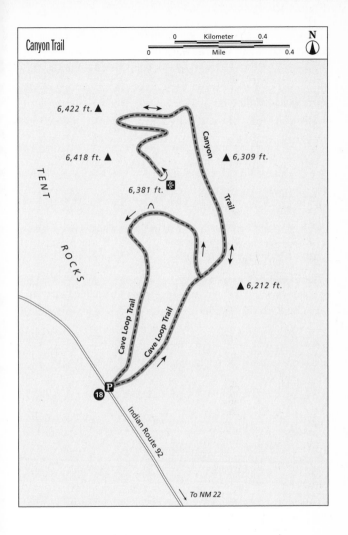

Canyon Trail

0   Kilometer   0.4

0   Mile   0.4

N

6,422 ft. ▲

6,418 ft. ▲

T E N T

R O C K S

6,381 ft. ☀

Canyon

▲ 6,309 ft.

Trail

▲ 6,212 ft.

Cave Loop Trail

Cave Loop Trail

P
18

Indian Route 92

To NM 22

in that they lack the crystalline structure of most solid minerals. Obsidian is formed during volcanic eruptions when surface lava cools rapidly, preventing crystals from forming.

Miles and Directions

0.0 Leave the trailhead and follow the right-hand branch of the Cave Loop Trail.

0.4 Leave the Cave Loop Trail and turn right onto the Canyon Trail.

1.4 Arrive at the viewpoint; retrace your steps on the Canyon Trail.

2.4 Turn right onto the Cave Loop Trail to continue the loop portion of the hike.

2.7 Arrive at the cave.

3.3 Arrive back at the trailhead.

19 Canada-Capulin Trail

This scenic, longer hike wanders through the Dome Wilderness in the Santa Fe National Forest and crosses several canyons on the way to a spring just inside Bandelier National Monument.

Distance: 7.4 miles out and back

Approximate hiking time: 5 hours

Difficulty: Moderate due to distance and elevation change

Trail surface: Dirt and rocks

Best season: All year

Water availability: None

Other trail users: Equestrians

Canine compatibility: Dogs on leashes allowed

Fees and permits: Permit required for overnight backpacking in Bandelier National Monument

Maps: USGS: Canada, Cochiti Dam

Trail contacts: Santa Fe National Forest, Jemez Ranger District, P.O. Box 150, Jemez Springs, NM 87025; (575) 829-3585; www .fs.fed.us/r3/sfe/districts/jemez/; Bandelier National Monument, 15 Entrance Rd., Los Alamos 87544; (505) 672-3861 ext. 517; www .nps.gov/band

Special considerations: During the summer, hike early or late in the day and carry plenty of water. During the winter, snow may linger on the shady north slopes.

Finding the trailhead: From the junction of I-40 and I-25 in Albuquerque, drive 32.9 miles north on I-25 to exit 267. Turn left onto NM 22 and drive 12.3 miles. Here NM 22 turns left; continue straight ahead on IR 90. Continue 4.2 miles, and then turn right onto IR 92. Drive 3.6 miles to the trailhead, which is just before a sharp left turn. GPS: UTM 13S 374796E 3952865N

The Hike

After leaving the trailhead, the Canada–Capulin Trail climbs a bit over a low saddle, then descends gradually to cross the first of three major canyons. After crossing Eagle Canyon, the Canada–Capulin Trail swings around a point and starts to descend the steep west slopes of Sanchez Canyon, the deepest canyon along the trail. The point where the trail crosses Sanchez Canyon makes a good turnaround point for those who want an easier hike.

After contouring below St. Peters Dome, the Canada–Capulin Trail meets the St. Peters Dome Trail. Continue straight ahead on the Canada–Capulin Trail and follow it generally northeast as it contours around minor drainages. The trail crosses several tributaries of Medio Canyon before finally crossing the main arm. After Medio Canyon, a short but steep climb leads to the boundary of Bandelier National Monument at a gate. After crossing an unnamed drainage, the Canada–Capulin Trail meets the short spur trail to Turkey Spring. Turn left here to visit the spring, the destination for the hike.

Much of the Dome and Bandelier Wildernesses were burned by a devastating wildfire in April 1996. Started by a campfire that was left burning, the fire raged for days and required more than 900 firefighters to contain it. Dry weather, low fuel moisture, and high wind caused extreme fire behavior. The charred trees are a stark reminder to be careful with fire, especially when the fire danger is extreme.

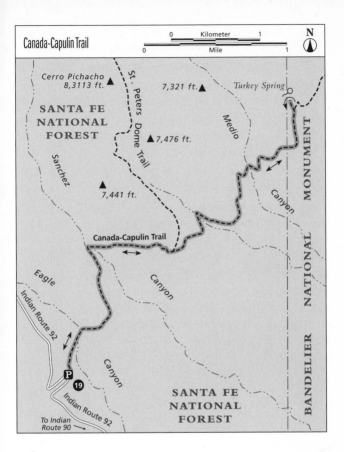

Miles and Directions

0.0 Leave the trailhead and follow the Canada-Capulin Trail.

0.3 The Canada-Capulin Trail crosses Eagle Canyon.

1.1 The Canada-Capulin Trail crosses Sanchez Canyon; this is the turnaround point for an easier hike.

1.8 Past the junction with the St. Peters Dome Trail; continue straight ahead on the Canada-Capulin Trail.

2.9 The Canada-Capulin Trail crosses Medio Canyon.

3.2 Pass the high point of the hike.

3.6 Leave the Canada-Capulin Trail and turn left onto the Turkey Spring Trail.

3.7 Arrive at Turkey Spring; return the way you came.

7.4 Arrive back at the trailhead.

20 Fourth of July Trail

This hike climbs past a spring to a scenic meadow in the Manzano Mountains. This is an especially fine hike in fall when the bigtooth maples are blazing with yellow, orange, and red leaves. The meadows along the crest offer stunning views.

Distance: 4.8 miles out and back

Approximate hiking time: 4 hours

Difficulty: Moderate due to elevation gain

Trail surface: Dirt and rocks

Best season: Spring through fall

Water availability: Upper Fourth of July Spring

Other trail users: Equestrians and mountain bikers

Canine compatibility: Dogs on leashes allowed

Fees and permits: None

Maps: USGS: Bosque Peak

Trail contacts: Cibola National Forest, 2113 Osuna Rd. NE, Albuquerque 87113; (505) 346-3900; www.fs.fed.us/r3/cibola/districts/mountainair.shtml

Special considerations: Trails may be snow-covered during the winter and early spring.

Finding the trailhead: From the junction of I-40 and I-25 in Albuquerque, drive 14.5 miles east on I-40, then take exit 175. Turn right onto NM 337 and drive 29.8 miles. Turn right onto NM 55, drive 3.2 miles to Talique, and then turn right onto Torreon Talique Loop Road, A013. Continue 7.0 miles to the Fourth of July Campground and park in the trailhead parking area. GPS: UTM 13S 373885E 3850588N

The Hike

From the trailhead, follow the Crimson Maple Trail around the west side of the campground, and then stay left on the main Fourth of July Trail, which heads west up the canyon.

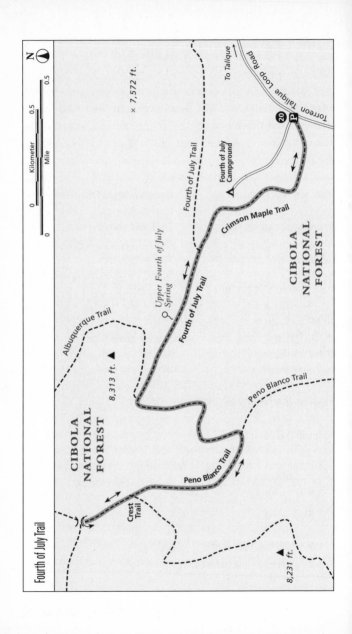

Fourth of July Trail

N

Kilometer   0   0.5
Mile   0   0.5

× 7,572 ft.

To Talique

Torreon Talique Loop Road

Fourth of July Trail

Fourth of July Campground

Crimson Maple Trail

20 P

CIBOLA NATIONAL FOREST

Fourth of July Trail

Upper Fourth of July Spring

Albuquerque Trail

8,313 ft. ▲

Peno Blanco Trail

CIBOLA NATIONAL FOREST

Peno Blanco Trail

Crest Trail

8,231 ft. ▲

A spur trail goes sharply right; stay left and continue west past Upper Fourth of July Spring to the junction with the Albuquerque Trail. Stay left and follow Fourth of July Trail as it swings south though a saddle, heads a drainage, and ends at the Peno Blanco Trail. Turn right and follow the Peno Blanco Trail northwest, where it meets the Crest Trail on a bench below the main crest of the Manzano Mountains. Now, turn right onto the Crest Trail and follow it north into a saddle with an open meadow. This scenic meadow is the end of the hike; return the way you came. (The Crest Trail ends about a mile north at the boundary of the Isleta Pueblo Indian Reservation.)

As you hike through the ponderosa pines, you'll almost certainly hear and see one of the pine forest's most distinctive residents, the tassel-eared squirrel. Also known as Albert's squirrel, these large squirrels have tufts on their ears, bodies about a foot long, and 9-inch tails. A slightly reddish back and gray sides further mark this rodent. The shrill warning bark made when hikers approach is unmistakable, and you'll spot them running across the ground to escape up the nearest pine tree, and then running along the branches high overhead.

Miles and Directions

0.0 Leave the Fourth of July Trailhead and start on the Crimson Maple Trail.

0.5 Stay left on the Fourth of July Trail.

0.6 A spur trail goes sharply right; stay left on the main Fourth of July Trail.

0.9 Pass by Upper Fourth of July Spring.

1.2 Reach the junction with the Albuquerque Trail; stay left on the Fourth of July Trail.

1.7 Turn right onto Peno Blanco Trail.

2.2 Turn right onto Crest Trail.

2.4 Arrive at the meadow in the saddle at the junction with the old Ojito Trail; return the way you came.

4.8 Arrive back at the Fourth of July Trailhead.

Clubs and Trail Groups

Continental Divide Trail Alliance
P.O. Box 628
Pine, CO 80470
(303) 838-3760
www.cdtrail.org

New Mexico Mountain Club
P.O. Box 4151, University Station
Albuquerque, NM 87196
http://pages.swcp.com/~nmmc/index.php

Sierra Club
Rio Grande Chapter
http://riogrande.sierraclub.org/

The Nature Conservancy
212 E. Marcy St.
Santa Fe, NM 87501
(505) 988-3867
www.nature.org/wherewework/northamerica/states/
newmexico/

About the Author

Bruce Grubbs has been hiking, cross-country skiing, paddling, biking, and climbing in the Southwest for more than thirty years. In addition to outdoor writing and photography, he is an active charter pilot. His other FalconGuides include these titles:

Basic Essentials: Using GPS
Best Easy Day Hikes Flagstaff
Best Easy Day Hikes Las Vegas
Best Easy Day Hikes Sedona
Best Easy Day Hikes Tucson
Best Hikes Near Phoenix
Camping Arizona
Desert Hiking Tips
Explore! Joshua Tree National Park
Explore! Mount Shasta Country
Grand Canyon National Park Pocket Guide
FalconGuide to Saguaro National Park and the Santa Catalina Mountains
Hiking Arizona
Hiking Arizona's Superstition and Mazatzal Country
Hiking Great Basin National Park
Hiking Northern Arizona
Hiking Oregon's Central Cascades
Joshua Tree National Park Pocket Guide
Mountain Biking St. George and Cedar City
Mountain Biking Flagstaff and Sedona
Mountain Biking Phoenix